C000125683

NATHANIEL HALL

Nathaniel Hall is a theatre-maker and HIV activist from Manchester. He writes, directs, inspires and produces bold and provocative, socially minded work.

He studied Theatre and Performance at the University of Leeds (Bretton Hall), graduating with First-Class Honours in 2008.

Nathaniel creates theatre and stories with (and for) people who are traditionally unheard or marginalised, and is an expert-by-experience in the art of telling autobiographical stories of health and well-being. He has delivered projects for Contact Theatre, the Royal Exchange Theatre, 20 Stories High, Wellcome, Trans Creative, Manchester Pride, George House Trust, the LGBT Foundation and Manchester University NHS Foundation Trust.

Nathaniel has lived with HIV since the age of sixteen and is a prominent voice in HIV activism, having told his personal story across many platforms, including on BBC Radio and Television News, MTV UK, Buzzfeed UK and *Attitude* magazine. He advocates for better representation of LGBTQ and HIV+ actors across the industry.

As a television actor, Nathaniel appears in *It's A Sin*, the Channel 4 drama about HIV/AIDS in 1980s Britain, written by Russell T Davies and first broadcast in January 2021.

He is Co-Artistic Director of Dibby Theatre and dad to two dogs, Peggy and Fred.

www.nathanieljhall.co.uk
@nathanieljhall
@DibbyTheatre

Dibby Theatre
in association with Waterside Arts

FIRST TIME

Nathaniel Hall

NICK HERN BOOKS
London
www.nickhernbooks.co.uk

A Nick Hern Book

First Time first published in Great Britain in 2020 as a paperback original by Nick Hern Books Limited, The Glasshouse, 49a Goldhawk Road, London W12 8QP, in association with Dibby Theatre and Waterside Arts

First Time copyright © 2020 Nathaniel Hall

Nathaniel Hall has asserted his moral right to be identified as the author of this work

Cover photography and design by Lee Baxter
Designed and typeset by Nick Hern Books, London

Printed in Great Britain by Mimeo Ltd, Huntingdon, Cambridgeshire PE29 6XX

A CIP catalogue record for this book is available from the British Library

ISBN 978 1 84842 976 5

CAUTION   All rights whatsoever in this play is strictly reserved. Requests to reproduce the text in whole or in part should be addressed to the publisher.

Amateur Performing Rights   Applications for performance, including readings and excerpts, by amateurs in the English language throughout the world should be addressed to the Performing Rights Department, Nick Hern Books, The Glasshouse, 49a Goldhawk Road, London W12 8QP, *tel* +44 (0)20 8749 4953, *email* rights@nickhernbooks.co.uk, except as follows:

Australia: ORiGiN Theatrical, Level 1, 213 Clarence Street, Sydney NSW 2000, *tel* +61 (2) 8514 5201, *email* enquiries@originmusic.com.au, *web* www.origintheatrical.com.au

New Zealand: Play Bureau, PO Box 9013, St Clair, Dunedin 9047, *tel* (3) 455 9959, *email* info@playbureau.com

Professional Performing Rights   Applications for performance by professionals in any medium and in any language throughout the world should be addressed to Nick Hern Books (address above).

No performance of any kind may be given unless a licence has been obtained. Applications should be made before rehearsals begin. Publication of this play does not necessarily indicate its availability for amateur performance.

Contents

Foreword
Paul Fairweather, lifelong LGBT and HIV activist

HIV has been part of my life, politically and personally, for over thirty-five years.

I have been active in campaigning around HIV since the earliest days of the epidemic. In 1985 I was one of six gay men who set up Manchester Aidsline, now George House Trust, and I have been living with HIV myself for over twenty years. Manchester has a long and proud history of HIV and LGBT activism and I've been there to witness much of it.

I remember the level of fear and hatred that existed in the early days of the epidemic all too well: Greater Manchester Chief Constable James Anderton talking about 'gay men, drug addicts and prostitutes swirling in a cesspit of their own making'; my friend Roger being forcibly held at Monsall isolation hospital (he was released only after we lobbied the council); the health service quarantining an ambulance because they thought it would give people AIDS... I could go on.

We picketed and shouted and educated whilst at the same time supporting our friends and lovers who were dying from AIDS. I could write a fabulous eulogy by my mid-thirties, not something I ever thought I would become so adept at before my retirement. I still take time to remember and celebrate the lives of all my friends who died so young. On 1 December each year (World AIDS Day) we remember those we have lost to the virus, but also commit ourselves to supporting those living with or affected by HIV across the world.

Today, the situation is very different: with medication, you can expect to live a normal lifespan. However, the stigma remains. Far too many people living with HIV feel isolated and alone, unable to tell anyone about their HIV status. *First Time* so clearly shows the psychological impact of being silent and the benefits of being open.

For the last three years I have managed the Positive Speakers project at George House Trust, working with an inspirational group of volunteers who tell their personal stories of living with HIV to school and college groups, staff training days, to student nurses and even to staff at GP surgeries. The power of this first-person storytelling, and their willingness to answer the frank and forthcoming questions that arise from it, cannot be underestimated in the fight against HIV.

Nathaniel Hall has been a Positive Speaker for many years. I first heard him tell his story to a group of teenage girls at a school in South Manchester. He read a letter he had written to his sixteen-year-old self telling him that despite the darkness and despair from the trauma of such a young diagnosis, his future would be full of amazing adventures. The creativity in his storytelling pre-empted the play he would go on to write, and the girls were still moved by his story and by how open he was at answering all their questions.

I have watched *First Time* with several different people living with HIV and have seen what a powerful impact it has had on all of them. Our stories and experiences differ hugely, but seeing the damage done by stigma and self-stigma is something we all could relate to. I felt a deep resonance with Nathaniel's story: navigating the stigma and shame of the diagnosis, I too delayed telling my family for many years, just like he did.

At the play's premiere in 2018, some of the other Positive Speakers and myself told our stories alongside Nathaniel onstage during a post-show discussion. The sell-out audience bristled with questions, insights and an electric energy that spilled out into the foyer and bar afterwards. We even received a standing ovation at the end, something I had never experienced before!

First Time has moved people with its truth and its humour. It's a show full of deeply important messages about health and well-being, about stigma and shame, but with so much creativity packed into seventy minutes, it never feels like a lecture.

We know that people living with HIV all over the world have been moved by Nathaniel's story. The play has been featured on mainstream TV, went viral on social media, has received critical acclaim and has won awards at the Edinburgh Festival Fringe. As a lifelong activist, I'm thrilled to see key public-health messages reaching such a huge audience.

The play and its coverage reflect the growing confidence of people living with HIV. For us, the U=U message (Undetectable = Untransmittable) is a powerful tool for eradicating stigma, one that clearly proves we pose no risk to others in terms of onwards transmission of the virus.

The U=U message is helping in the fight against stigma and self-stigma. More and more we are speaking out, talking to our friends, family and colleagues about living with the virus, and what that means for our lives.

I'm certain that *First Time* will continue to be used as a catalyst for change and I'm delighted to be working with Nathaniel as a key partner of *In Equal Parts*, a creative community outreach project tackling HIV stigma and shame that has been inspired by the show.

I hope you enjoy reading the play, laugh and cry as you do so, but above all I hope it inspires you to challenge HIV stigma and live boldly and with pride in your own lives.

Paul Fairweather is the Positive Speakers Coordinator for George House Trust and former councillor for Harpurhey, Manchester.

Introduction
Nathaniel Hall

First times are scary, aren't they?

In 2018 I said something out loud for the first time. It was
utterly terrifying. After fifteen years of living in secret, I came
out to the world a second time. You see, the first time I ever had
sex, aged sixteen, I contracted HIV. Let me take you back to the
summer of 2003...

I was Head Boy at my comprehensive high school in Stockport,
and I wasn't out; in fact, I even had a girlfriend. But this Head
Boy was also secretly giving head... to the Deputy Head Boy,
no less. You know, I was desperate to go to the prom with him
on my arm, but Stockport in 2003 really wasn't ready for that,
so a cream tuxedo was the next best thing. But it hadn't arrived
at the hire shop... two hours to wait in STOCKPORT. *What a
depressing place...*

I sat on a bench overlooking the shopping precinct to the M60
beyond. And that's where I met him. He was older than me,
mid-twenties maybe, tanned, bleached tips in his hair, ripped
bootleg jeans... definitely gay. We chatted. It was validating.
We swapped numbers, texted each other on our Nokia 5210s.
He was so sweet, and my age wasn't an issue to him, although,
looking back, I think perhaps it should have been.

Eventually we went back to his for my 'first time'. He pulled out a
safer sex pack but just took the lube. I stopped him, I may have
grown up under the shadow of Section 28, but I wasn't stupid. He
reassured me, a clean bill of sexual health, and I trusted him. After
all, it was my rite of passage; he was older and wiser, surely?

My fate was sealed.

I found out I was HIV+ two weeks before my seventeenth
birthday. Just a child, now forced into a very adult world. Then

I boxed up what had just happened and put it high on a shelf. I told a few lovers, fewer friends, no family. Until fourteen years later in 2017, I caught myself in the mirror still awake two days after a house party. You see, I'd convinced myself I was simply living my best queer life: parties, sex, alcohol, drugs. All fun things if you're actually pursuing them for fun. Not so much if you're pursuing them to mask pain. You know, I look around at my community that is supposed to be celebrating pride, but behind closed doors so many of us are drowning in shame.

And who can blame us?

Throughout history we've been medicalised, criminalised, dehumanised, erased, beaten, tortured, killed. And now we're emerging from one of the worst epidemics to ravish civilisation in recent history: 35 million people dead, 38 million (and counting) living with HIV, and my community, men who have sex with men, disproportionately affected. On the road to freedom and equality, it sometimes feels like one step forwards, two steps back, and it was so easy for them to weaponise this disease to fit their own hate-filled agenda.

'Britain threatened by gay viral plague.' '"I'd shoot my son if he had AIDS," says vicar.'

Real headlines from the British tabloid press at the height of the early AIDS crisis.

And more recently, on the front page of a national paper in 2016: *'£5000 a year lifestyle drug…what a skewed sense of values,'* they scoffed as they pitted access to PrEP (life-saving medication that stops people contracting the virus) against access to statins for old people (thankfully, after years of campaigning, PrEP is now available for free on the NHS in England, Scotland and Wales).

I was diagnosed with HIV aged sixteen, but it was the stigma and shame, not the virus, that led me to breaking point.

Staying silent about an HIV diagnosis only confirms to others that it is something to be ashamed of. It took me over a decade to get here, but let me tell you one thing right now…

It. Is. Not… Regardless of how you caught it.

When I caught a glance of myself in the mirror on that fateful day in 2017, I realised I had bought into the narrative of stigma, and in that moment I made a pact with myself to change the narrative, and to keep shouting the new narrative until people would listen. That was the catalyst that set the wheels in motion to create *First Time*.

But first I had to tell my family that for the past fifteen years I had held such a huge secret from them. It was a good job I did, because nothing could have prepared me for what was about to come…

I was commissioned to write and perform the show by Waterside Arts in Greater Manchester, in association with Dibby Theatre, in the lead-up to World AIDS Day 2018. And that's when the press picked up the story. I performed four sell-out shows amidst a whirlwind of interviews for newspapers, magazines, television and radio.

Something about my story struck a chord with millions.

Even if they didn't have HIV themselves, it unlocked parts of their own lives where they held shame, and for those with HIV, many finally felt relief at seeing an honest portrayal on their screens and stages. It was clear to us that the full impact of this show was yet to be made, so we took it to the Edinburgh Festival Fringe in 2019 and then on a national tour. It won two awards and enjoyed audience and critical acclaim in equal measure. From alcohol and drug-fuelled rock-bottom to award-winning writer and performer in the space of two years, it's been one hell of a journey.

But *First Time* is more than just a play. It's part of a growing confidence in the HIV community to live boldly and without shame. More and more people are talking openly about their diagnoses and, very slowly, the stigma is being removed from the virus.

I have used *First Time* as a vehicle for my HIV activism with creative workshops, outreach and education sessions in schools, charity partnerships, rapid HIV testing at venues and fundraising parties. *In Equal Parts* – a community-led creative outreach project tackling HIV stigma and shame – is now helping more and more people with their diagnoses and reminding all of us that we have a role in ending HIV.

I know, that as a white, cis-gendered male from a comfortable background, I write all this from a position of privilege, and that, for many people living with HIV, coming out publicly is simply not an option. So I've vowed to keep on telling my story – on their behalf – until it is safe for them to do so themselves. HIV healthcare has changed (find out how in this book!) and is revolutionising the lives of people with HIV. And now another revolution is on the way: a generation of people not just living with HIV, but thriving with it.

You know, I'm really one of the lucky ones… I survived.

People often remark that what I'm doing is 'remarkable' and 'brave' but it's not. Ordinary people do extraordinary things every single day. I'm just a kid from Stockport hoping for a day when saying you're HIV+ is no longer considered a radical act.

Acknowledgements

First and foremost, thank you to Chris Hoyle and Ross Carey –
my rocks throughout this journey – and to my friends Ciara
Tansey and Adam Laidler for your unwavering support and
love.

Thank you to Paul Fairweather and the Positive Speakers at
George House Trust, Colin Armstead, Neal Sharpe, Greg
Thorpe, Emma Zurowski, Dr Bella Starling, Darren Adams and
the staff at Waterside Arts and Creative Industries Trafford,
Richard Evans, Tarrick Wilks, Tess Farley, Amy Vreeke, Matt
Fenton, Chloe Courtney, Stephen Hornby, Adam Zane, Rob
Ward, Kate O'Donnell, Carl Austin-Behan and Tom Ross.

Thank you to the organisations that have supported the project:
George House Trust, LGBT Foundation, BHA for Equality, HIV
Scotland, Terrence Higgins Trust, Superbia, Manchester Pride,
Venues North, Contact, the Lawrence Batley Theatre, Mother's
Ruin, 20 Stories High, Heald Green Theatre Company.

Thank you to all the #HIVHeroes who donated to our
#FirstTimeTour crowdfunding campaign. With special thanks to
John Lucas, Julie Hesmondhalgh, Russell T Davies, Carl
Austin-Behan, Chris and Steve Hall for your significant
contributions.

Special thanks to Saul Bromberger and Sandra Hoover
Photography and the staff and patients of Bailey-Boushay
House (1992–95) for allowing use of their images of HIV care
in the production.

A Poem

The following poem, also called 'First Time', formed part of the early development of the play. It was first performed at Mother's Ruin, Manchester, in 2018.

My first time was with Sue
Everything was brand new
Not exciting but nervous
Was my first time with Sue.

The place where it happened felt clinical
Sue came across a bit cynical
Like she'd seen my type before.
But she was accommodating and kind
Everything you'd expect to find
From your first time.

It was painful that first time
I remember it blind-
-sided me in a way I didn't expect
And up the tears crept
As Sue entered abruptly
Took my breath
Touched me
On the hand, then the face.

I'd expected an embrace
From my first time
But this one kept it purely professional
Listened to my confessional
Then offered me a tissue
To clean up the mess that I'd just made on her desk.

I never did see her again
All I have left is the memory when
I had my first time with Sue.

My second time was with Carol
Who dressed in fancy apparel
Which made it a little more relaxing
For a second time with Carol.

The door this time was closed,
Much better for a supposed
Intimate exchange of details
With a little red light above as if to say:
'STOP! Don't enter this way'
It all felt a little bit naughty
Like we were up to something saucy.

Well, I remember she did have rather large fingers
That could bring us
To a quick and satisfactory conclusion
Not one for illusion
Or romance was our Carol.
Maybe a brief chat
About the weather or the bus
Never one to fuss…

But I liked her cardigan with the chunky knit
And her boisterous Northern charm and wit
It helped to ground me
On my second time with Carol.

My third time was with Karen,
In a room so utterly barren
That I started to get depressed
On my third time with Karen.

Now, Karen was married to Darren,
A fact she mentioned every time
I entered her barren patch.
If I had a dime
For every time…
I'd be rich… in America at least.
Karen was my least favourite
And not because she was unfriendly but –
She liked to talk and keep things light

And sometimes it really felt like she might
Turn it into something meaningful and special.
But in the end it was always a dis-appointment

In the room that was ever so barren
Talking to the woman who was married to Darren
On my third time with Karen.

My fourth time was with Andy
Now Andy... was bit randy
In a way that was utterly inappropriate
For a fourth time with Andy.

You see,
Andy had cottoned on that I was a bit of an old-timer in this place
He could tell that I'd graced
The presence of many before him.
And so, he'd perch right on the rim
Lean really close in
And ask all the usual
But in a tone that suggested he wanted a little bit more:

'Condoms for you today?
A leaflet off the carousel about which ways
Make it more comfortable and fun, perhaps?'

Whoa! No thanks, Andy!
You've collapsed the whole illusion
Of the conjugal collusion
I've created here in my mind.
Only I'm allowed
To make wild assimilations
Of words and smut.
Tut tut, Andy, tut tut.

To be honest
It was all rather unprofessional
In the place of the confessional
Was my fourth time with Andy.

My fifth time was with Janet,
Dammit, Janet! was from another planet

And not one in this galaxy either
Such was my fifth time with Janet.

Now, Janet never made me feel relaxed
Calm
In fact my palms
Often sweated in her presence.
I now of course
Was well-versed
In this exchange
Nothing could embarrass or upset
But we mustn't forget
That other-planet-Janet was new...
And shit.

My times with Janet were bumbling
Fumbling
Pre-pubescent encounters
Full of misunderstandings,
Double bookings
Unanswered phone calls
And constant lookings for this and for that.
I feared greatly for anyone who
Had the unfortunate to-do
Of Janet as their first time.

In the end my patience was lost
And I snapped wildly at her boss
Which ended my fifth time with Janet.

My sixth time...
I can't remember
Well, let's face facts
It gets less special
Each time.

You see, my whole adult life has been spattered,
With well-meaning folk
Who go home at the end of the day shattered
From first-time encounters
And fat fingers that move fast

From telling the same story
And sounding aghast
On the punch line
From making inappropriate innuendo
Just to make the day go quicker
And from being thrown in at the deep end
In cost-cutting exercises
Designed to make services that little bit slicker.

And I'm sad that I've forgotten their real names and their faces
That I've reduced them to stock characters
Without airs and without graces
Or the detail that each human being deserves
Simply for saying warmly:

'Come in, have a seat, love,
No need to be concerned
Six months again then, pet?
Those CD4s'll be in the 500s then, I'll bet.'

And whilst for them it's just a job
They never forget
That for you each visit
Is plagued with regret
And remorse
And with guilt
And with anger.

Which all melts away
When first-time Sue comes out with a clanger:

'Be with you in a minute, love,
I've just gone arse-over-tit in the lube cupboard.'

And you smile
And you sigh
Even through tears
Looking back through the years
The impact she'd have, you never even knew
When you had that first time, that first time with Sue.

A Context

HIV healthcare has changed, but people's knowledge of the virus – and attitudes towards those living with it – still lag behind.

HIV is treatable: people on successful treatment cannot pass on the virus and in 2018 the UK became the first Western nation to meet the UN's targets on reducing infections.[1] Cities across the UK are also signing up to become HIV Fast Track cities, committing to reducing new transmissions to zero by 2030.[2] And with the introduction of PrEP, more people on effective treatment and better HIV health campaigns, leading HIV charities believe that we now have the tools to end HIV in a generation.[3]

But there are thousands of people with HIV across the country who live in fear of people finding out.

Recently, several media outlets claimed a man 'risked his life' having sex with his HIV+ girlfriend so they could have a baby when there is in fact no risk as she was on effective treatment. And in 2016, the *Daily Mail* ran a front-page headline claiming that HIV medication was a '£5,000 lifestyle drug' implying that money shouldn't be spent on preventing people getting HIV over other life-saving health interventions, such as statins for older people.

Sadly, worrying and stigmatising headlines like this aren't uncommon. They add fuel to the fire that people with HIV are a danger to others, which contributes to a culture of fear that stops people getting tested regularly. *First Time* aims to educate,

---

(1) theguardian.com/society/2018/nov/29/uk-meets-un-target-end-hiv-epidemic-unaids-public-health-england

(2) who.int/hiv/pub/arv/wad-2015-infographic/en

(3) lgbt.foundation/news/lgbt-foundation-welcomes-progress-on-ending-all-new-transmissions-of-hiv-within-a-generation/248

destigmatise and empower, in turn contributing to the aim of ending all new transmissions of HIV by 2030.

A Glossary

HIV (Human Immunodeficiency Virus)
A virus that attacks the immune system, present in bodily fluids. Transmitted though unprotected vaginal and anal sex, blood to blood (e.g. sharing needles) and mother to baby during birth/breastfeeding (this last way is rare thanks to screening and medication).

AIDS (Acquired Immunodeficiency Syndrome)
A collection of illnesses caused by the collapse of the immune system as a result of untreated HIV. Today, an AIDS diagnosis does not mean a person will die for certain, many people recover with treatment. A highly stigmatised term.

Advanced HIV
A less-stigmatised term now often used in place of AIDS.

CD4
A type of cell in the immune system that HIV attacks and uses to replicate itself. In other parts of the world CD4 cells are known as T-cells.

Viral load
The amount of HIV in a HIV+ person's blood.

Undetectable viral load
When the amount of HIV is below forty copies per millimetre cubed of blood, a person is 'undetectable'.

Anti-retrovirals/combination therapy
The medications used to treat HIV.

PEP (Post-Exposure Prophylaxis)
Medication given to a person who may have been exposed to HIV, which can stop them becoming HIV+. Available on the NHS in the UK.

PrEP (Pre-Exposure Prophylaxis)
Medication taken pre-emptively if a person may be exposed to
HIV, which can stop them becoming HIV+. Available on the
NHS in the UK.

U=U (Undetectable = Untransmittable)
A person who has been on HIV treatment for over six months,
whose viral load is 'undetectable', cannot pass the virus on to
others.

For up-to-date information on HIV in the UK always seek
advice from reputable websites. We recommend:

www.tht.org.uk
www.ght.org.uk
www.nat.org.uk
www.hiv.scot

A History

First Time was commissioned by Waterside Arts and Creative Industries Trafford and was developed in association with Dibby Theatre.

It was first presented by Dibby Theatre and Waterside Arts at Waterside Arts on 29 November 2018. It subsequently enjoyed a critically acclaimed run at Summerhall during the 2019 Edinburgh Festival Fringe, where it was awarded the Venues North Edinburgh Fringe Award and the VAULT Pick of Summerhall, and was named in *The Stage*'s Best Shows at Edinburgh Fringe 2019.

The production has toured to Hull Truck Theatre, Touchstones Rochdale, Shout! Festival Birmingham, VAULT Festival London, Stephen Joseph Theatre Scarborough, Harrogate Theatre Royal, York Theatre Royal, the Garrick Lichfield, the New Adelphi Salford, Northern Stage Newcastle, Theatre in the Mill Bradford, the Dukes Lancaster, Harlow Playhouse and Curve Leicester. It will tour again nationally in 2021.

Writer and Performer	Nathaniel Hall
Director and Dramaturg	Chris Hoyle
Designer	Irene Jade
Original Music and Sound Designer	Nathaniel Hall
Live Art Consultant	Stacy Makishi
Lighting Designer	Joel Clements
Additional Sound Design	Joel Clements
Marketing Design	Lee Baxter
Trailer	Georgiana Ghetiu
Trailer Animation	Gavin Wood
Production Photography	Andrew Perry, Lee Baxter, Dawn Kilner and Youcef Hadjazi
Technical Stage Manager	Joel Clements

PR Consultant	Rachel Furst
Marketing	Nathaniel Hall
Producer	Ross Carey
Producer for Dibby	Chris Hoyle
Executive Producer	Nathaniel Hall

Supported with grants from Arts Council England, Waterside Arts and Creative Industries Trafford.

The original development of *First Time* was seed-funded with a grant from Superbia, the arts and culture fund from Manchester Pride.

Dibby Theatre

Dibby Theatre is an award-winning touring theatre company from Manchester that tells urgent and untold stories full of Northern wit, grit and soul that celebrate the diverse community they serve. LGBTQ-led, they are activists with a shared desire for social change. They tell their own stories and support other to tell theirs in their own way too.

Their debut production of *The Newspaper Boy* (2018) by Chris Hoyle received critical acclaim and enjoyed a fourteen-night sell-out run as part of Queer Contact 2018.

Dibby Theatre are Chris Hoyle (Co-Artistic Director), Nathaniel Hall (Co-Artistic Director) and Ross Carey (Producer).

@DibbyTheatre

Waterside Arts

Waterside is a thriving and vibrant arts venue in the heart of Sale in Trafford. Comprising a theatre, art galleries, studios and workspaces, the centre is an important regional hub for both performance and visual art.

www.watersidearts.org | @watersidearts | Insta: @watersidearts_

Creative Industries Trafford (CIT)

CIT is the artist-development strand at Waterside Arts, established at the venue in 2004. The project provides talks, masterclasses, opportunities and mentoring for artists working in animation, literature, theatre and visual arts.

www.creativeindustriestrafford.net | @citrafford | Insta: @creative_industries_

Photograph Credits

1. Revisiting the real bench in Stockport whilst filming the trailer
2. Moment 3: A Cream Tuxedo, a Will Young Lookalike and a Fucking Depressing Place
3. Moment 4: A Prom, a Proposal and a Vauxhall Astra
4. Moment 4: 'A life that would never be'
5. Moment 4: 'The winner's song moment'
6. Moment 5: A Disco, a Dodgy Tummy and a Coming Out (of Both Ends)
7. Moment 6: Diagnosis
8. Moment 9: A Pill-Popper's Cabaret
9. Moment 11: PTSD-TV
10. Moment 13: A Vigil to Remember (That I Survived)
11. Moment 14: Funny How a Story Comes Full Circle
12. In Equal Parts workshop

Photos 1 and 12 by Nathaniel Hall, 2020.

Photos 2, 3, 7, 8, 9 by Andrew Perry of the Edinburgh Festival Fringe production, 2019.

Photos 4, 6, 10, 11 by Dawn Kilner of the original production, 2018.

Photo 5 by Youcef Hadjazi of the Edinburgh Festival Fringe production, 2019.

7

8

9

10

11

12

FIRST TIME

To Mum and Dad –
Sorry it took me so long to say it out loud

Character

NATHANIEL, *early thirties*

The play is set in the present day.

A large neon-light triangle (3m x 3m x 3m) dominates the back of the stage – during the show it changes colour to suit the scene.

(The original production featured a 6m-wide glitter curtain with pink triangle motif in place of the neon-light triangle.)

It is reflected on the floor with a taped pink triangle that reaches its point at the front of the stage.

They are reminiscent of the pink triangle that the Nazis used to identify gay men – later reclaimed by ACTUP activists in the 1980s.

In front of the neon triangle is a park bench with a park bin next to it.

There is a red heart-shaped balloon tied at one end of the bench.

The bench is partially covered with a duvet, concealing the balloon.

Above is a mirror ball.

There are four envelopes suspended stage-left – each one has a letter on them:

H.

O.

P.

E.

They are too high to reach.

Stage-right, a hospital screen.

Stage-left, a rail of clothing.

Also onstage: two small stage blocks painted with bright eighties motifs and a microphone on a stand.

There's been a party: confetti, popped balloons, streamers, empty cups and bottles litter the stage and the auditorium.

Throughout the play, more and more mess is made.

At intervals, this is swept up or piled around the bin.

Everything in this play is true. Some names have been changed to protect identities.

Pre-show:
I'm Not Ready

As the house opens, the stage is empty.

We can see a pair of legs sticking out from under the duvet which is tossed over the bench – someone is asleep on the floor.

The remains of a party are littered across the stage – burst balloons and paper cups.

The stage doesn't look beautiful like it should before a show – the lights are yet to be powered up.

After a short while, and whilst the audience are still entering the space, the legs begin to move and a young man, NATHANIEL, emerges, wearing a grey dressing gown and a bright-coloured bum bag.

His hair is wild and he has white powder around his nose – he's clearly been partying and is the worse for wear.

As he comes round, he notices people are being let into the space.

He frantically addresses them.

The following is ad-libbed and improvised live, his energy is chaotic, comedic but also with a hint of tragedy – he is clearly not in a good way.

Shit! Shit! Fucking shit!

No, no, no, no.

You can't come in!

Shit, I feel asleep.

Erm, no stop, wait!

My worst nightmare.

We had a party last night…

Erm… shit.

Okay.

Okay, you can let them in I guess.

I'm not ready but… oh Christ, look at the state of me.

Is it that time already?

Just need to clean up this mess.

I'll just have a quick whip-round.

He grabs a bin bag and starts to tidy some rubbish from the auditorium.

Anyone seen the Hoover?

Directly at someone in the audience who is giving him disapproving looks:

Oh yes, hello!

Haven't you ever been to a party?

Let loose?

God, whose idea was it to do this in [venue name or area]?

Gang of stuck-up bastards.

He gestures to the technician's box.

Joel, can we get some music on?

Loosen this lot up a bit.

'Club Tropicana' by Wham! plays.

He dances a bit.

Oh, that's much better, get the party started again.

He spies something (or does he smell it?) and makes a beeline for it: a small drugs bag with some white powder in that has been left by a partygoer.

Ooh, someone's left a baggie.

He gives a look: Shall we/shan't we?

Be rude not to, it's Christmas soon, isn't it?

He counts the people in the room.

One, two, three... thirty... sixty-two... ninety.

Looking at the bag – it's clearly not enough.

Not quite the feeding of the five thousand, but I'll give it a go!

He sniffs the powder in one go.

Sorry, did you want some?

The ad-libs continue as the audience grows and he repeats the key information people need to know:

Sorry, wasn't ready, went out last night and had a party.

(*Holding up the baggie.*) Getting the party started again.

Yes, don't mind the mess, come on in, take a seat.

At some point the drugs very visibly kick in – he stops and stares straight ahead as they course through his veins.

Once everyone is seated, we segue to...

Moment 1:
The Morning After the Night Before

The audience are in and the signal from Front of House is given directly to NATHANIEL.

He looks confused.

Then he realises that means it's time to begin.

His energy is frenetic – it's funny but we see he is really struggling, physically and mentally – he's in the middle of a mental breakdown.

That everyone?

Best make a start then, Joel.

The music fades and the lights dim.

(Referencing the lyrics of 'Club Tropicana'.) Free?!

FREE?!

Have you ever been to Pike's Hotel in Ibiza?

That's where the music video was filmed.

Thirteen euros for two lemonades.

Twelve quid for a bit of fizzy pop.

I said, we're certainly not in [local gay bar or club] now, are we, Toto?

He pulls out a gin bottle and takes a swig.

It's a good job I always carry a back-up in my bum bag, for emergencies.

Oh, it's real gin by the way.

He drinks the whole bottle – Wowee, that's strong!

He moves the two boxes into place, one stage-left, one stage-right, ready for the show to start.

Sorry about the mess.

We went out last night.

Everyone came back here.

Things got a little bit messy.

Still managed to miss my get-in.

He spies some keys that have been left.

Oh, someone's left their keys.

Oh, they've got a Waitrose Partner card, fancy!

Maybe it was that producer that's been hassling me for a blowjob on Grindr?

I never did put out, in case you're wondering.

I may look like a total trash-bag, but I grew up in Cheshire, thank you very much.

Ah, well, you snooze, you lose.

He licks off the 'gear' left on the keys and grimaces at the bitter taste.

Erm, it would appear I've lost track of time a bit.

This is awkward.

I've not really prepared anything.

I've only had two years, a commission, two grants from the Arts Council, an award-winning run at the Edinburgh Fringe, and a successful crowdfunding campaign...

It's just hard to make a start, you know?

But this is it!

You're all here, waiting to hear about my 'First Time'!

He sniffs some white powder that he has pulled out of his bum bag – until the action of the sniff, he is unaware he is doing it, it's second nature.

He looks at the audience and quickly puts the powder away.

You know, I had a nightmare about this.

In it, no one's turned up except my mum, which is good because I haven't learnt the lines.

So, I'm reading off the script, when Mum gets up and goes to leave and as she's leaving, she says: 'Not your best, good job no one came.'

He breathes in deeply and stares manically at the audience.

This isn't the dream, is it?

I did make a start on the script, promise.

But I got distracted by listicles.

You know what a listicle is, right?

A series of pointless facts with a catchy headline aimed at distracting you from doing what's really important:

'Fourteen Hidden Signs Your Boss Secretly Hates You.'

I can tell you in one – you're a cunt.

'Ten Surprising Signs You're Having a Mental Breakdown.'

Pause – that's a bit too close to home.

I didn't like the sound of that one.

I did print one off though.

He pulls it out of his bum bag.

'Fifty-five Fascinating Facts for Serial Procrastinators.'

Well, if the boot fits.

(*Reading.*) 'Number one: Female kangaroos have three vaginas.'

(*Aside.*) I wouldn't even know what to do with *one*.

'Number two: The oldest condoms ever found date back to the 1640s…'

Says here they were found in a cesspit in Dudley Castle.

He crumples the list up and throws it in the bin.

Who was it that said that thing about cesspits?

Sir Cyril James Anderton, former Chief of Greater Manchester Police.

(*Sarcastically.*) He was a lovely chap.

Good Christian man.

You know what he said back in the eighties when a mysterious illness decimated my entire community?

You know what he said?

He said: drug addicts, prostitutes and homosexuals were 'swirling around in a human cesspit of their own making'.

He looks down at himself and wipes white powder from his nose – pot, kettle, black.

Pause.

His daughter came out as a lesbian a short while after.

Nice to see the universe still has a sense of humour.

He crosses the stage when suddenly…

Moment 2:
An Interruption from the Theatre Gods

A loud boom as a harsh spotlight hits centre-stage.

NATHANIEL *is trapped. The theatre gods are forcing him to confront what he's been putting off for so long.*

A voice-over is heard – it is his own voice.

He can hear the voice too and reacts accordingly.

(*Voice-over.*) That's me.

Baby number 26,276,907.

Born on the NHS.

A responsible and productive member of British society...

Oh, who am I kidding?

This is not me at my best, folks.

This is my Britney-circa-2007 moment, although it's actually 2017 and I haven't shaved my hair off... yet.

If I'm honest, it's been a long time coming.

A light illuminates the suspended letters.

I have written something, but it's not for you.

HOPE – it's just four little letters.

He is looking at the suspended letters.

It's only taken me fourteen years to do it.

Look, I don't make a habit of taking drugs in the middle of the day.

A pained expression, he cleans his face up with his sleeve.

But believe it or not, this is the moment that changed my life.

And I was off my box, two days after a house party, googling kangaroo vaginas.

A small, apologetic curtsy.

So yeah, that's me for you.

I'm not explaining myself very well.

Let me show you instead.

He pulls the duvet cover off the bench revealing a red heart-shaped balloon – it hovers in the middle of the neon triangle.

A beat, then…

Moment 3:
A Cream Tuxedo, a Will Young Lookalike and a Fucking
Depressing Place

Music plays: 'Ice Cream' by Leo Rossa.

NATHANIEL *moves to stage-left, his bedroom/dressing area, and takes off the dressing gown, cleans his face, neatens his hair and puts on a school bag. We are heading back in time to his teenage years.*

He walks up to the bench – the neon triangle lights up a bright daytime blue. He sets the scene:

June 2003, early afternoon.

Stockport.

A bench overlooking the shopping precinct to the M60 beyond.

Overcast.

He sits on the bench.

School is out.

It's the summer people say is the best of your entire life.

It's the day of the prom.

But the tuxedo I want hasn't arrived.

Everyone wears black but I'm the Head Boy and I want to make a statement in cream.

Secretly I'd rather make a statement walking in with the Deputy Head Boy on my arm.

We've been sucking each other off in the attic for the past few months.

But two guys going to prom together?

Stockport in 2003 really isn't ready for that shit.

I'm not out yet, but I'm not far off.

So, a cream tuxedo is the next best thing.

But it hasn't arrived at the hire shop.

Next delivery is 4 p.m.

Two hours to kill.

Two hours…

…in Stockport.

What a fucking depressing place.

Pause. He looks about, bored, then reaches into his bag and pulls out a Nokia 5210 mobile phone.

Sit for a while.

Play *Snake 2* on my phone.

Text the Head Girl.

She's my date for the night even though I have a girlfriend, it's just the done thing.

He notices someone sitting down next to him on the bench – it makes him uncomfortable, but he's curious too.

A guy sits down.

He's older.

Not like *old*-old.

Mid-twenties, maybe.

And he's got a meal deal from Boots.

He looks over.

Look away.

An awkward smile.

He starts to eat.

'I think I stole too much,' he says.

Stole?

'Well, I don't steal it all.'

'You see, the cashier only scans the paper bag, so if you pack it carefully you can get two of everything in but only pay three pounds.'

'Do you want some? I've got a chicken and stuffing sandwich going spare.'

He passes the sandwich.

And this time I get a proper look.

He snatches a glance and – oh my god, he's really fit!

He's the spit of Will Young, and he has a slight lisp just like him too.

He's tanned.

Bleached tips in his hair.

Ripped bootleg jeans.

Definitely gay.

Like, visibly gay.

And confident about it too.

It's exhilarating.

A gay man, being really fucking gay… in Stockport!

'What are you doing in Stockie?' he says.

Waiting for a cream tuxedo, it's my prom tonight.

Pause – that wasn't the response he was expecting.

Then he says:

'Look, I don't normally do this, but I couldn't help but come over, you seem really nice and, well… fit.'

'Do you want to swap numbers?'

He's not as confident now.

He's worried I'll say no or call him a creep or run off and part of me wants to but instead I say:

Erm, yeah, why not?

I put my number in his phone, all the while thinking this is the worst idea in the history of ideas:

I've just met a stranger on a bench, eaten a stolen chicken and stuffing sandwich off him, and now I'm giving him my phone number?

Every inch of my inside is screaming: *What the hell are you doing?*

But he's gay...

Circa-2003 gay, but still, a real out-and-proud gay man.

And he's picked me.

A final coy smile.

He stands and goes to leave, crossing in front but then he stops – the man has called after him:

'You've only put your number in, what's your name?'

Nathaniel.

'Nice to meet you, Nathaniel. I'm Sam.'

Moment 4:
A Prom, a Proposal and a Vauxhall Astra

Music plays: 'Ice Cream' by Leo Rossa.

NATHANIEL *leaves the bench, beaming from ear to ear, and returns to the dressing area.*

He gets ready for the prom: a mirror, hairspray (taken from the stage-left box), a bit more hairspray, a lot more hairspray – he coughs in the cloud of spray – and then finally, a cream tuxedo.

The latter is put on with almost church-like reverence.

He looks at the audience – Oh yeah, I look gooooood.

He goes to put on more hairspray, hesitates, then does it anyway.

He leaves his bedroom and enters the prom – the neon triangle glows pink.

I made it to the Head Girl's house with about two minutes to spare, necked a Blue WKD, posed for a photograph and jumped in the limo to the prom.

Considering we'd been talking about it non-stop for the last year, it was bit of a disappointment.

Some photos, a meal, *one* glass of wine – watch the cream tuxedo – some more photos and a disco.

Countless 'I'll miss you's and 'Let's stay in touch's.

None of them genuine.

Well, mine weren't at least.

The end of the night.

The dreaded last dance.

Everyone's partnered up.

I look about for the Deputy Head Boy.

And a brief fantasy sweeps through my head and for a moment we're dancing together right under the mirror ball and everyone is looking on, shocked and confused.

It's interrupted as I catch sight of him in a dark corner necking Janine Bailey.

Little does she know.

He mimes giving a blowjob.

I get a tap on the shoulder.

It's the Head Girl: 'May I?' she jokes.

'You may,' I joke back.

He addresses the audience directly.

Now, I can't possibly recreate the last dance at my prom all on my own, so I'm going to need a female-identifying volunteer from the audience to help me out.

The lights in the auditorium come on and he chooses someone from the audience.

They go into hold directly under the mirror ball.

He ad-libs as he does so: Can you remember your last dance at your prom? You didn't have one? Oh, that is sad isn't it, folks! Well, we're making memories tonight! You put your hand here and I'll put mine here if that's okay? Whoa, not too close, nice safe distance.

He stares into the audience member's eyes.

I looked at her as we assumed the position.

And I looked *straight* into a life that would never be: a proposal, marriage, kids… (*With absolute dread.*) a Vauxhall Astra.

The lights dim.

They do.

The mirror ball starts spinning.

It does.

And the music plays…

Music plays: 'Evergreen' by Will Young.

…and it's only 'Evergreen' by Will bloody Young.

A fantasy sequence ensues with the volunteer from the audience.

We see the heteronormative life that could have been:

He pulls out a small silver box, gets down on one knee and proposes.

He holds up a sign: 'She said "Yes!"''

He takes a veil out to try on his blushing bride… but puts it on himself instead.

They walk down the aisle together and get married as he sobs.

He runs over to the bin, looks in and then pulls a doll out of the bin and throws it to her – It's a boy!

He pulls another doll out of the bin (feigned happiness/dread) and throws it to her – It's a girl!

He pulls two more dolls out (this time real dread) – It's twins!

He goes to throw them, but clearly they won't be caught so he aborts – Just messing, I wouldn't throw our kids!

He sits his new family down on the bench.

Unsure what to do with the two new babies, he shoves them underneath the bench, hoping his blushing bride won't notice, before pulling a car registration plate out of the bin that says: 'Just Married.'

His wife sits next to him holding two of their newborns and the happy couple are about to set off for a life of long drives in the Vauxhall Astra when…

Suddenly, a needle scratches and the music stops, as we hear the screech of tyres from the Vauxhall Astra speed off into the distance.

Snapping out of the fantasy sequence:

That's not my life.

Sorry.

(*To his new wife*.) It's not you, it's me.

You can sit back down now.

He ushers the audience member back to their seat.

(*Referring to the babies*.) No, take them with you... you can have full custody.

He mimes: Phew! Close call.

The last dance comes to an end, the lights come on, and everyone starts to make their way home when:

The sound of a Nokia 5210 text message.

He pulls the phone out of his pocket and looks at it.

It's from Will, I mean Sam:

'How's the prom going, handsome? Wish I could slow dance with you.' Winky face.

And I'm saved!

'Evergreen' by Will Young plays again, this time at the big key-change moment.

A confetti cannon bursts.

It is like being shot straight through the heart.

It hurts.

He stumbles, but then...

It's first love.

It's validation.

It's the winner's song moment.

It's EVERYTHING.

And he wants to make it evergreen so it will last forever.

He walks out of the prom into the night and sits on the bench where he met Sam – the neon triangle turns a dark blue.

The music fades.

You know, he was criticised for singing that song to a girl, because he was gay.

It was a big thing back then, coming out.

That was the first text of many.

Sam and I set off on a whirlwind romance from his high-rise apartment in Stockport.

Alright, it wasn't much, but it was *my* first time.

We perved at the presenter on *Cash in the Attic* and the fit GP in the soap *Doctors* during marathon daytime TV sessions.

And we sat and chatted about anything and everything.

They say it's the best summer of your life...

And I wanted to make it evergreen.

He tosses the phone in the air in celebration, catches it and heads to his dressing area, as...

Moment 5:
A Disco, a Dodgy Tummy and a Coming Out (of Both Ends)

Music plays: 'The Summer of Love' by Steps.

NATHANIEL *takes the tuxedo off and removes his black T-shirt to reveal a brightly coloured vest – we're going on holiday – he pulls out comedy tropical sunglasses and a mirror-ball drinks-holder cocktail from the stage-left box.*

He has a new-found confidence in his burgeoning sexuality, but he's still not 100% comfortable just yet.

The neon triangle turns a deep evening-sunset orange.

August 2003, Menorca.

It's hot.

European-heatwave hot.

I've had a dodgy tummy for a few days and felt a bit 'off'.

Mum thinks it's something I've eaten and this incessant heat.

It's my last holiday with my parents and my little sister.

My two older brothers have already flown the nest.

My sister is eight and is obsessed with Steps.

I've been living my best queer life vicariously through her 'reluctantly' learning the routines when she begs me to.

I'm no longer in the closet though.

Mum sat me down and asked me if I was gay…

He sits on the stage-left box in a harsh spotlight.

I said I thought I was bi.

And when she asked why, I said the pull of the Vauxhall Astra was strong.

She just looked at me confused.

'If you're worried whether God still loves you then...'

Mum!

She's a good Christian woman.

Not the crazy conservative type though.

She once said 'cunt' at the dinner table.

Then she said:

'Me and your dad know about Sam. We think he's too old for you.'

My bum fell out a little bit.

'And have you been using condoms?'

MUM!

We had a bit of sob together on the sofa.

And after she'd gone, I text Sam.

She was right, he was too old.

The spotlight goes and we're back in Menorca – that deep sunset orange is back.

So, we're on holiday.

My sister has tired herself out learning the routine to 'Summer of Love' with the holiday animation team.

So Dad goes back to the room with her in his arms.

Music plays underneath: 'Asereje' by Las Ketchup.

'There's a disco on tonight if you fancy a dance.'

Mum likes to dance.

I've had a few parent-approved alcoholic drinks so I'm feeling loosened up and ready to go.

Oh, and the song of the summer is on.

The music swells and suddenly we're at the disco.

The neon triangle flashes in bright colours.

'Come on then, show us what you got!'

(*Mouths.*) Sorry, she's so embarrassing.

Mum!

He dances.

Nervous at first.

Then more confident.

Soon he's nailing it – the proper Las Ketchup routine!

But then something is not right.

The music distorts – we're going under.

The room spins and before we know it, he is being sick.

The sick is silly string.

It goes over someone in the audience.

'I'm so sorry.'

More sick.

Then – Oh god please no – diarrhoea.

He pulls his pants down round his ankles and bends over, but it's too late.

Silly string fires out of his arse all over someone in the audience.

'Sorry, oh god, it went in your drink/hair!'

It's going everywhere, making a complete mess.

He tries to clean up the mess.

The colour is draining from the whole space.

We're no longer on holiday any more.

This isn't fun.

In fact, this is really serious – Stop laughing, why are you all laughing at me?

Where am I? Why are my pants round my ankles? Oh god, more sick…

It's every teenager's worst nightmare.

The sequence ends with him violently retching over the bin.

He looks up at the mess that's just been made.

They say it's the best summer of your entire life.

He is sick again, an awful gut-wrenching sound.

He spits the vomit out and lets out a painful whimper.

He looks at the audience, a tear in his eye:

What a fucking mess.

A beat, then…

Moment 6:
Diagnosis

A clock ticks loudly.

NATHANIEL *wipes the sick from his mouth and readjusts his clothes, then slowly moves over to the hospital screen stage-right.*

We can hear other sounds associated with a clinic – murmured talking, a phone ringing.

He is clearly very anxious.

November 2003.

The GUM clinic waiting room at Stepping Hill Hospital.

I didn't get much better after the holiday, in fact I spewed so much out of both ends I lost over a stone.

Mum took me to the emergency doctors the day we landed – a waterborne virus.

The virus passed and I started college, but I was still sickly and had a nasty cough.

Then the seepage started, down below.

Thick, green seepage.

So I took myself to the clinic.

He steps into the role of a nurse:

(*Bright and breezy.*) Gonorrhoea, non-specific urethritis and genital warts.

A pained expression.

They offer the big test.

I refuse.

(*Remembering.*) You could back then.

But the doctor calls me back and insists.

He sits on the stage-right block in the waiting room.

The end of Cash in the Attic *is heard from a TV screen.*

He watches.

It's quiet.

A couple of TV screens play daytime TV – *Cash in the Attic*.

Next up, *Doctors*.

Running away from the waiting area is a long corridor full of doors.

Doors to examination rooms, counselling rooms, a toilet with a hatch to a small lab so you can piss in a cup and pass it through.

There's a water cooler but there aren't any cups.

There are never any cups.

There's a small table full of information leaflets, everything from 'Gonorrhoea' to 'Good Vaginal Hygiene'.

They're not in neat piles – feels like whoever tries to keep them neat has given up.

There's another table with bowls of condoms and sachets of lube and little paper bags to fill up and take away, a sort of adults' pick and mix.

And at one end, red ribbons and a suggested donation box.

The opening credits to the daytime soap Doctors *are heard coming from the TV.*

He watches and waits, nervously, a child in a very adult world.

As he speaks the following, he opens the box and pulls out items to dress up as an NHS Health Advisor called Sue.

He escapes into fantasy to distract from what is really happening.

Why do people even watch this crap?

Except for that bit of eye-candy, Dr Green.

I mean, the script is terrible.

And the storylines?

Well, it's not *Casualty*, is it?

Bit of mild diabetes?

It's hardly life or death.

It's actually just a light comedy really.

Sometimes it's a total farce.

I mean, take her for instance, the receptionist.

She's just playing it for laughs.

They're always dead mumsy too.

The NHS Health Advisors, that is.

They're always called Jackie… or Carol… or Janet… or Sue.

He is fully dressed as his drag alter-ego Sue: big 1980s glasses, a polyester cardigan, and blonde wig.

She is Northern, camp, funny, but full of kindness – exactly the person you want around when you hear bad news.

SUE.   Sorry about the wait, love, just went arse-over-tit in the lube cupboard.

It is Nathaniel, isn't it?

Hiya, love, do you want to come through?

She walks away and makes small talk during which she blows up latex gloves and puts them on.

A spotlight forms on the bench where he met Sam – she speaks as though that is where he is sat listening.

How've you been?

You've just started at college, haven't you?

How you finding it?

Ah, it's great you're enjoying it.

She pulls out an oversized syringe, unsettling sounds bubble up – this is really going to hurt.

>So, we've got your test results back and I'm afraid to say, they're…

She bursts the balloon with the needle. BANG!

There is an ear-piercing ringing.

The neon triangle strobes bright white light like a flickering striplight in a horror film.

We hear the chorus of 'Evergreen' by Will Young, but it is echoey and distant.

He stumbles, dazed and confused: Why am I dressed like this?!

He pulls the items off and struggles to stand.

He drags himself into the place where he met Sam, into the spotlight.

He takes off Sue's wig and glasses and stares straight ahead, reeling from the what he has just been told.

Tears begin to form – No, no, no, this isn't happening.

The sound builds until it is almost unbearable but then stops abruptly as he takes a sharp intake of breath.

Heavy breathing.

He looks up into the harsh spotlight and blinks.

Where am I?

Then straight to the audience:

What a fucking mess.

A beat.

He pauses, unsure what to do next.

Where do we go from here?

Moment 7:
A List of Things That Happened After Diagnosis (in No
Particular Order)

A sudden burst of activity.

NATHANIEL *frantically takes Sue's cardigan off and throws it*
over the bin – I don't want to be in this memory any more.

He looks about the stage, lost, scared.

Then a moment of decisive action – No, I'm in control here.

He brings a microphone on a stand centre-stage in a harsh
spotlight.

It's the one from earlier, it's almost blinding.

He takes a piece of paper off the stand – a list that he is about
to read to us.

There's no more pretense or playing – we see the real
Nathaniel, not the performed NATHANIEL.

His tone is matter-of-fact, confessional – These things happened
to me.

A list of things that happened after diagnosis, in no particular
order.

I went home on the bus.

I tried to tell Mum and Dad.

I cried a lot.

I thought I'd never be able to have children.

I got drunk and went missing for a whole night in Sydney.

I went to university and got a degree in Theatre and
Performance.

I text a guy that I'd been flirting with and told him – he became
my first proper boyfriend.

I started to make myself sick as punishment.

My close friend died suddenly, aged thirty-two – he was buried in a Disney-themed coffin.

I got a hug off Fiona.

I didn't blame Sam.

People at my old school found out and rumours started spreading that I had HIV.

I blamed myself.

I sometimes would drink too much because it helped ease the pain.

I cheated on my boyfriend.

My boyfriend cheated on me.

I tried to tell Mum and Dad.

My sister developed epilepsy.

I consoled countless people who cried when I told them I had HIV.

I overcompensated by trying to be perfect at everything.

I nearly died in a thunderstorm and flash flood in Australia.

One of my housemates left the gas on and I nearly died, again.

I went to an illegal rave in a field.

I went to a sauna.

I went to my brothers' weddings.

I sat in silence when some friends made jokes about AIDS.

I tried to tell Mum and Dad.

I cried the day after.

I became an uncle.

I became a vegetarian.

I found out Thatcher's homophobic Section 28, the law that stopped schools openly talking about homosexuality, was repealed in 2003.

I got depressed.

A pause – this one is hard to admit.

I smashed a plate-glass window.

I got through a lot of condoms and lube.

I nearly got pneumonia.

I voted to Remain.

I unintentionally locked my best friend in the living room, and she had to climb out the serving hatch.

I had homophobic abuse hurled at me whilst shopping for dog food at Pets at Home.

I tried to tell Mum and Dad.

I took drugs and had a great time.

I tried to tell Mum and Dad.

I took drugs and had an awful time.

I tried to tell Mum and Dad.

I hated myself.

I tried to tell Mum and Dad.

I tried to tell Mum and Dad.

He turns to a new page – the same sentence is just repeated over and over on the page.

I tried to tell Mum and Dad.

He looks at the letters above him.

A deep breath.

He strikes the microphone as…

Moment 8:
Drugs Make Things Better, Right?

Music: an original composition plays, emotive 1980s synths.

NATHANIEL *heads back to the dressing area and puts his dressing gown back on – this one has been pre-set with bags of pills concealed in the pockets.*

He takes out a pot of medication and a bottle of gin (bigger than the first one) from the stage-left box.

He sits, tired, sad, reflective.

You know, that night I got home from the clinic I lined up some paracetamol.

Oh, I was never going to do it.

Ever the drama queen.

I wasn't prescribed anti-retroviral medication until 2008, about five years after I was diagnosed.

He shows the bottle and takes out a tablet – it looks almost too big to swallow, just like the real thing.

I was prescribed Atripla.

Hailed as an 'HIV wonder drug'.

The first ever once-a-day tablet.

No more fistfuls of pills, like I'd seen in the movie *Philadelphia*.

The first time I took it, it made me hallucinate.

Made me sweat so much you could ring out the towels I had to sleep on.

Each night was the same: lucid dreams, vertigo, night terrors.

The doctor was right though, the extreme side effects did subside after a couple of weeks.

But not completely.

Every few nights I'd wake up screaming.

And it messed with my head: paranoia, anxiety, self-doubt.

I'd keep having these nightmares about Will – (*Correcting himself.*) I mean Sam.

He holds the pill up again and stares at it.

It was hailed as a HIV wonder drug, but it wasn't.

Not for me.

Not for a lot of people.

I don't take it any more.

A new once-a-day tablet came onto the market a short while after.

But it cost the NHS thousands of pounds more than older medicines.

So a panel of people I'd never met had to decided I was worth it.

He remembers something is in his trouser pocket.

He pulls it out.

It's a drugs baggie with an oversized white pill in it.

A guilty, knowing look – old habits die hard.

Other 'drugs' proved useful, to help me forget.

At least for a short while.

Until you come crashing back to reality.

God, I started treatment eleven years ago.

I wonder how many pills I've swallowed since then?

Moment 9:
A Pill-Popper's Cabaret

Music plays: 'Leave Right Now' by Will Young.

NATHANIEL *looks at the Atripla pill, it's time to take it.*

After a brief moment he pops it into his mouth.

But what to swallow it down with?

Ah, the gin – Cheers, everyone!

He looks at the white pill in the drugs bag, then at the audience.

A pause.

Then: What the hell, let's push the 'fuck it' button.

He swallows it with a big swig of gin, this time it really burns.

He looks at the pot of pills: Is it time to take another one already?

He stands up and pulls a bowl and spoon out of the box – this will be easier.

He pours Atripla pills into the bowl and tosses the bottle on the floor.

He stands on the box, takes a large spoonful, but before they reach his mouth an idea stops him in his tracks.

He reaches into his pocket and produces a small baggie with white powder in – Seasoning, what a great idea!

He sprinkles it on his pill breakfast somewhat manically.

He scoops up a mouthful on the spoon, goes to eat, spots a judgemental eye from the audience, stares them out, then mouths 'What?!'

He shoves the concoction in his mouth and chews.

The pills are licorice torpedoes and they make his mouth and spit turn black.

He chews and takes another large mouthful.

He begins to cry.

But then he finds more pills in his pocket – this time a giant oversized baggie full of brightly coloured ones.

In the bowl they go.

He is scooping them into his mouth with the spoon, his hand… anything.

He begins to lip-sync to the track: 'I think I better leave right now, before I fall any deeper…'

Pills and spit tumble out of his mouth.

Another oversized baggie full of different pills.

The bowl is overflowing.

He is choking on the pills as he stuffs them in his mouth.

Another oversized baggie, this time full of white powder.

He throws the powder into the bowl and in his mouth as he tries to lip-sync.

He is making a complete and utter mess.

As if he hasn't got enough to try and swallow, he finds another bottle of pills.

The music swells.

He reluctantly lifts them high above his head and pours them into his mouth in silhouette.

But there is no room and they just go everywhere.

He is bent over double, crying at the state of himself.

It's utterly heartbreaking.

He stands and looks at the audience as the music comes to an end.

With a mouth full of chewed-up pills:

What a fucking mess.

Moment 10:
Whose Fault Is It?

NATHANIEL *takes a moment to pull himself together – the show must go on, no matter how painful.*

He picks up a discarded bag and spits out the 'pills' into it.

He looks at the audience shamefully, he can't believe he's allowed them to see him like this.

A flourish of decisive action – Remember, I'm in control here.

He takes off the dressing gown and wipes his face with it.

He gets a broom and sweeps up the mess he has just made – we're heading to the end of a support session at the charity George House Trust.

The neon triangle turns bright white like overhead striplights.

Everything is swept into a pile by the bin: pills, confetti, surgical gloves, the syringe, even the babies, an echo of a memory of a life that never was.

He takes a moment to gather himself.

I first went to George House Trust, a HIV support charity in Manchester, in 2010.

I'd kind of avoided it before that, if I'm honest.

I thought it would be all 'circle therapy' like in the musical *Rent*.

But I met other people living with HIV for the first time.

We shared stories over coffee and biscuits.

And with their support, I wrote a letter to my sixteen-year-old self as a way to process what had happened.

We'd go out to schools and staff training days and the like to tell our stories and I'd read my letter.

I was shocked at how little people knew about HIV and people's attitudes to people with the virus.

So I made it my mission to educate, destigmatise and empower.

And when we'd go to schools, we'd do a quiz with them – giving them the education I should have had aged sixteen.

Now, every day is a day for learning so let's have a go at a few little questions, shall we?

A flurry of activity.

He repositions the hospital screen to become a playing board for the quiz.

There are eighties gameshow-style picture cards that are hung on the screen as the quiz progresses.

This is a more theatrical version of the quizzes he now does whilst volunteering.

I've created a quiz for you all tonight.

It's a little bit more 'adult' than the school's edition.

Okay, it's pretty simple.

Each round I'll reveal two scenarios and you've all got to shout out which one you think is the highest risk for contracting HIV.

Got it?

Don't worry if not, you'll get the hang of it as we go along.

Okay, kicking us off tonight is…

He reveals an oversized playing card with keys in a bowl on it.

> 'It's keys in the bowl,
> shagging twenty people at a sex party.'

Told you it was a bit more 'adult' than the school's edition, sorry, Mum.

And we're comparing that with…

He reveals an oversized playing card with a stereotypical married heterosexual couple in love on it.

> 'Having unprotected sex with your loving husband
> who says he's HIV negative.'

Okay, if you think you are more likely to get HIV shagging twenty people at a sex party, shout out 'I love orgies' – and if you think you are more likely to get HIV from your loving husband, shout out 'I love my husband'.

Three, two, one, GO!

The audience are most likely to shout out 'I love orgies'.

Ad-lib: Crikey, you're a sexed-up lot, aren't you? Lots of orgy lovers in tonight!

But I'm afraid the correct answer is actually 'I love my husband'.

You see, I've not given you the full story...

Turns out...

Your husband arranged the sex party.

I'm sorry you had to find out this way.

You see, folks, two-thirds of all new infections come from people who don't know their HIV status.

And if he's lying about cheating, he's probably lying about getting tested.

Oh, it is sad when that happens.

Anyway, moving on...

Let's reveal the next two scenarios.

Oh, it gets worse... much worse.

Kicking us off is...

He reveals an oversized playing card with a picture of 'Jan from Accounts' on it.

> 'It's sex with Jan from Accounts!'

That free prosecco at the Christmas party doesn't half make you frisky, hey, Jan?

So that's our starting scenario.

And we're comparing that with...

He reveals an oversized playing card with a picture of a man in a gimp mask.

'It's sex with DirrrtyBarebackSexPig1986.'

And no, that is not my Grindr profile name.

Okay, so if you think you're more likely to get HIV having sex with Jan from Accounts shout 'No more prosecco for Jan' – and if you think you're more likely to get HIV from DirrrtyBarebackSexPig1986 shout out 'I'm a sex pig'.

Three, two, one, GO!

Most likely a mix of answers.

Ad-lib: You know what I heard there? Jan's a sex pig... which is a revelation!

But really it doesn't matter because like before, you've not been given the full story.

That's right...

Jan could be riddled with STIs because she's never been tested.

In fact, Jan's never had an HIV test in her entire life, because Jan thinks people from Accounts don't get HIV.

And whilst DirrrtyBarebackSexPig1986 might not be using condoms, he's actually taking PrEP – the drug that is 98% effective at stopping you contracting HIV.

What's more, he couldn't get it on the NHS trial in England, so he decided to buy it himself.

Looks like Jan from Accounts could learn a thing or two from DirrrtyBarebackSexPig1986.

Okay, on to our final two scenarios...

Kicking us off is...

He reveals an oversized playing card with a picture of himself on it.

'Unprotected sex with hottie who tells you they have HIV.'

Oh, it's me!

And we're comparing that with...

He reveals an oversized playing card with a photo of Phil Collins on it.

'Sex with Phil Collins using a condom.'

A short blast of Phil Collins singing 'I can feel it coming in the air tonight' (from 'In the Air Tonight').

I bet you can, Phil.

Okay, so if you think you're more likely to get HIV having unprotected sex with me, shout 'Nathaniel's a sexy beast' – and if you think it's condom-protected sex with Phil Collins shout out 'I love Phil Collins'.

Three, two, one, GO!

Ad-lib: Surprising number of Phil Collins' lovers in tonight. I won't tell.

Anyway, it doesn't really matter what you shouted out, because like the other two, you've not had the full story.

You see, your HIV+ bit of hot stuff – me – is actually undetectable.

Because I'm on effective treatment and my viral load is undetectable, the risk of transmission is reduced by 100%.

Undetectable = Untransmittable.

That's right, in terms of people in this room, where HIV is concerned, I'm the safest person you could be having sex with.

I bet some of you didn't know that now, did you?

He tidies the quiz cards away.

After the quiz, someone living with HIV would stand at the front and tell their story and then people could ask them questions.

Soon, I was confident enough to tell my story in the form of the letter I'd written to my sixteen-year-old self.

I was firing on all cylinders.

Until one day a hand went up and a question was asked...

A harsh spotlight shines on him as he gestures to the person at the back asking the question.

(*A voice-over with echo.*) Yeah, but wasn't it your fault you caught HIV?

It takes him completely by surprise – it's like having the wind kicked out of him.

He doesn't answer.

That high-pitched ringing fills the space again.

His new-found confidence disappears, he stumbles and looks lost, confused and scared again.

Moment 11:
PTSD-TV

NATHANIEL *goes and grabs the duvet, the bowl of pills and bottle of gin, and sits stage-left, wrapping himself up for comfort and safety.*

The high-pitched ringing continues – it's incessant and painful.

As the scene progresses, discordant synth music plays – it's dark, distressing, sinister and gets progressively louder.

Some days I was firing on all cylinders.

Not every day though.

The space is dark and isolating.

He can't shake the ringing off.

There was something strangely comforting about going back to that place.

That dark, drug-induced place.

That mind-numbing, mindless daytime-TV-*Cash-in-the-Attic-Doctors* place.

He finds a remote and clicks on the TV – an uplight flashes, casting nightmarish shadows across his face and the stage.

He picks up the bowl of pills from earlier and sits and munches on them like TV snacks.

He clicks through the channels.

It's harmless at first, but then the drugs kick in and things stop making sense, there is incessant static and distortion.

We hear what is on each channel:

The Cash in the Attic *theme tune…*

… static…

… the Pop Idol *theme tune…*

…static…

…Ant and Dec presenting the Pop Idol *final: 'And the winner is… Will, Will, Will, Will!'…*

…static…

…Margaret Thatcher at the Tory Party conference: 'Children who need to be taught to respect traditional moral values are being taught that they have an inalienable right to be gay'…

…static…

…the 1987 Government Public Health 'Don't Die of Ignorance' advertisement: 'There is now a deadly disease that is a threat to us all'…

…static…

…the dark sounds intensify, and that high-pitched ringing is getting unbearable.

He is gurning and twitching from the drugs and is paranoid.

The shadows make him jump: Who's there?!

This is about as traumatic as it gets: PTSD-TV.

But he is transfixed – no matter how dark this gets; he can't stop himself watching.

He describes what he sees, the memories that play on the TV screen:

I keep watching this scene.

We're at Sam's flat.

We've just had sex.

The first time.

He's suggested I have a bath to clean up.

I'm sat there, pale, skinny, sixteen years old – not a child, but not quite yet an adult.

And he's knelt next to me, most definitely an adult, sponging my awkward, pale skin.

But he didn't have a shower, so that didn't seem odd.

Is that right?

I'm sat in the bath and he's sponging me down with a flannel?

Why was he sponging me down?

He was smoking a cigarette.

No.

I'm sixteen?

And he's sponging me down?

A very dark realisation dawns on him.

As an adult, this doesn't look like he remembers it.

(*On the verge of tears.*) I thought it was romantic?

He tries to convince himself he's overthinking it.

TV shows are always more dramatic than real life.

It's just memories of memories that have been played and replayed and have got mixed up with too many box-set binges on Netflix.

That's what it is…

Let's just go back and check.

He rewinds and watches again.

Eyes wide.

The true horror of the memory comes across his face.

He doesn't want to look, but he can't stop it, it's like he's under a spell: No, no, no, no, no, no!

His body twitches and contorts.

He sweats.

He tries to escape but he can't.

I thought it was romantic?!

He rewinds it again and watches – the sound intensifies.

(*Unconvincingly.*) TV shows are always more dramatic than real life, right?

He rewinds a third time and watches.

The sound rises again – the noise is unbearable.

No, no, no, no, no.

Just switch it off.

Switch it off, just switch it off!

He tries to switch it off but the remote isn't working.

Why won't you switch off?!

He bangs the remote against his head repeatedly.

He tries it again, but it's still not working.

He is trapped, horrified – this is one hell of a bad trip.

Please just switch off, please, please, please!

There's someone in the room.

And someone over there.

They're coming to get him.

It's terrifying.

He screams at the television:

JUST FUCKING SWITCH OFF!

The plug is pulled.

Blackout – complete darkness.

Heavy breathing.

Moment 12:
'To Sue'

The heavy breathing continues in darkness – the light slowly returns.

NATHANIEL *is confused: Why am I sat here? Why is this remote in my hand? Why am I sweating?*

He has come around from the bad trip.

He stands and backs away from TV, looking at it intently, confused, horrified.

What just happened?

He looks up at the audience.

He is ashamed again: Sorry.

Sorry.

He gathers his thoughts.

I never did find out whether Sam knew or not.

Our lives went separate ways and we lost touch.

We saw each other at the clinic a few years back, so at least I can assume he's getting treatment.

I waited outside for over an hour.

But he never showed.

Must have left by a different door.

That was the last time I saw him.

He spots part of Sue's costume from earlier.

You know, I bet you all think this show's title is about him, Sam, don't you?

But my first time was actually with Sue.

Don't laugh, it's true.

It was special, although I didn't realise it at the time.

He takes Sue's clothes from the floor by the bin and hangs them on the hospital screen, taking extra care with them – he's realised how special people like Sue really are.

He steps back and looks at the memory of Sue.

I'm sad, that I've forgotten her real name and her face.

I'm sad I've forgotten all their names and faces.

They saved my life.

Sue saved my life.

He pulls out a tube of personal lubricant and squeezes some onto two fingers.

He recalls the memory of Sue:

'Sorry about the wait, love, just went arse-over-tit in the lube cupboard...'

A pause, then a look to the audience:

Oh, that actually happened.

He holds up his lubed fingers...

To Sue.

... and then sucks the lubricant off with a cheeky grin.

Moment 13:
A Vigil to Remember (That I Survived)

*Music plays: 'Angels, Punks and Raging Queens' from the
musical* Elegies for Angels, Punks and Raging Queens.

NATHANIEL *takes 'Sue' and hangs her on his dressing rail
stage-left.*

*He puts on a smart black coat with a red AIDS ribbon on the
lapel.*

He looks in the mirror and places his hand on the ribbon.

The neon triangle turns a deep night-time blue.

The sound of rain.

He picks up an umbrella and heads to the vigil.

Manchester Pride, Summer 2012.

It's the Monday after the Big Weekend.

The party is over.

Five thousand partygoers descend on Sackville Gardens to
remember those we've lost to HIV and AIDS.

This year they're going to hear my story in the form of the letter
I wrote to my sixteen-year-old self.

I've been reading it to groups of people for a while and George
House Trust had asked me if I wanted to read it onstage tonight,
but I can't because, well –

He looks at the letters hanging above the space.

But I said they could use my letter if it was anonymous.

So we changed my name and passed the letter to the director.

It was Adam Zane, someone I'd worked for previously.

I get a phone call:

'Hi, Nathaniel. It's Adam Zane here. I'm directing the candlelit vigil at Pride again and I've been given this gorgeous letter from a young gay lad who got HIV the first time he ever had sex. Thing is, he's not fully open about it yet, so we need a shit-hot actor to read it out on his behalf and I immediately thought of you.'

Fuck.

I made some lame excuse about volunteering all weekend.

At least he thought I was 'shit-hot', right?

So I'm at the front of the entire crowd in the VIP section.

It's Manchester, so, of course...

A crack of thunder, then more rain.

He opens the umbrella; it lights up with fairy lights.

A sea of umbrellas is forming behind me, hundreds upon hundreds.

All here to listen to *my* story.

The vigil starts.

A few speeches from important people.

Then it's my turn, I'm up.

A young man walks onto stage and takes the mic.

And I instantly recognise him: Rob Ward, an actor I met when working for Adam fucking Zane.

Seriously, trying to stay in the HIV closet is hard.

I compose myself as he reads the letter... (*Introspectively.*) my letter.

A short pause, he watches and listens as his letter is read out.

As he was reading it, I saw people holding one another.

Some were crying quietly.

One man was sobbing uncontrollably.

And that's when it hit me.

I SURVIVED.

I FUCKING SURVIVED.

So many queer men didn't.

So many died horrible, painful, lonely deaths.

They died as outcasts.

They died and so many people thought they deserved it, simply because they loved another man.

When Rob got to the bit about the NHS and everything it has done for people like me, the crowd just went wild.

Five thousand people celebrating our country's greatest achievement, celebrating their own personal Sue.

And in that moment, I was reminded of photos I'd seen from the early AIDS wards.

You know, a friend of mine who was there, right at the height of the epidemic, he told me guys on the wards used to give each other handjobs under the covers.

Life finds a way.

Love finds a way.

By this point in the proceedings, I am blubbering mess.

Full-on-snot crying.

But I compose myself, just in time for the candles.

Music plays: 'Youth' by Daughter.

He picks up two small silver boxes.

Now, under the seats at the ends of the rows there are some silver boxes.

If you would like to take a candle and pass them down.

Now is the time to light them.

Everyone in the audience takes out electric tealight candles and switches them on.

The space is filled with twinkling light.

He moves the hospital screen centre-stage.

Once everyone is ready with their candles, he stops and looks out, recalling the five thousand people at the vigil.

A deep breath, this bit is really hard for everyone, but we're going to get through it together.

Now's the time to remember the 35 million people who have died from AIDS.

Now's the time to stand in solidarity with the 38 million people who live with HIV.

Now's the time to give thanks, that each and every day you wake, you've survived.

The crowd goes quiet.

And a sea of candles burns brightly, each of them for someone, somewhere.

The music swells.

He joins the crowd at the vigil and watches the stage as a series of black-and-white images from the early AIDS wards is projected onto the screen. The people depicted are a range of different ethnicities.

A busy day-care centre with men and women nursing their brothers and lovers.

A mother lovingly holding her painfully thin son with a smile of contentment and peace on her face.

A family visiting in the hospital, the mother feeding her baby, an uncle holding his niece.

A woman nursing a man on a drip on a couch.

A man cleaning his partner's sores.

Two men in a loving embrace, with life continuing on the busy street outside.

A man with sores around his mouth staring deeply into the camera.

Another man in a tender embrace with his gaunt and dying partner.

A family celebrating a birthday on the ward with cake, candles and happy smiles.

A woman left all alone in her bed.

A mother and father nursing their emaciated adult son in bed with his childhood teddy bears surrounding him.

And finally, an empty, neatly made hospital bed.

The music fades as it finishes.

A pause for as long as is needed to find the strength to speak.

I survived.

He slowly makes his way back to the stage.

An act of care for his audience:

Now, is everyone okay?

Does anyone need a tissue?

He offers someone in the audience who is crying a tissue.

I've only got one, so you'll have to share it out amongst yourselves.

Relief – we got through it together, just.

(*To himself.*) It's okay.

Moment 14:
Funny How a Story Comes Full Circle

NATHANIEL puts down the umbrella and moves the hospital screen stage-right back to its original position.

The lights slowly grow to daytime – the neon triangle a bright, light blue.

He is melancholic and reflective.

It's sad that Mum and Dad weren't there to experience that moment with me.

I tried to tell them so many times.

It was just three little letters after all.

But they just wouldn't come out.

So eventually I just stopped bothering.

Some days I even forget I'm positive.

Relief – another story to distract us from doing what needs doing to get to the end of the play:

But that doesn't last long when you're single.

I've had years of dating disasters.

One guy said it was morally wrong if someone with HIV didn't declare it before sex.

I said, 'Why not slap a pink triangle on the lot of us and be done with it?'

They weren't all bad though.

He was living in Liverpool and working in Manchester and I was doing the opposite.

Our GPS signals met somewhere in the depths of rural Cheshire and…

There is the sound of a Grindr message notification.

... 'Look, I need you to know before this goes any further, I'm HIV+.'

'So am I.'

Before him, I always had to use protection.

He was my first time without.

He grabs the rucksack and makes a journey back to the bench.

The clinic at the hospital closed a few years back and moved to the centre of Stockport.

Right across the street from the bench where I met Sam.

Funny how a story comes full circle.

He sits and remembers.

He finds a photograph in his bag.

It's him at the prom, aged sixteen.

He looks at it for a moment.

Music plays: 'Evergreen' by Will Young.

Me at the prom.

Go on then, you can have look.

He shows it to some people in the audience.

The party that's supposed to kick-start the rest of your life.

Some days it feels like the party was over before it even began.

He places the photo on the bench.

He takes an envelope with 'Dear Nathaniel' written on the front out of his rucksack.

He places it underneath the photo on the bench.

He takes a Boots chicken and stuffing sandwich out and places it next to them.

He closes his bag.

He sits and looks at the little shrine he has left.

The music swells and the lights fade.

It's emotional, but perhaps a little bit too saccharine sweet.

The show's over, folks…

But then…

Moment 15:
Another Interruption from the Theatre Gods

Suddenly the bright spotlight and loud boom from earlier interrupt.

NATHANIEL *glares into the light, blinded.*

He tries to hold the moment – this isn't supposed to be happening, has someone got the cue wrong?

He mouths: No, no, no!

A voice-over, his voice again – like before, he can hear it and reacts.

He desperately gestures to cut it, pull the plug, but it continues to play, and he is forced to listen.

That's me.

Baby number 26,276,907.

Born on the NHS.

Still delaying.

Still 'playing for time'.

Times up, kidda.

Got to face up to the real truth.

The hard truth.

You fucked it up.

That's not the real ending, is it?

Stop trying to fool them.

Spotlight's on you now.

Do the right thing.

It's time.

Turn those three little letters into four.

Moment 16:
It's Just Four Little Letters

NATHANIEL interrupts the voice-over, all pretense is lost, it's just Nathaniel onstage now.

He has exhausted every theatrical delay-tactic possible – nowhere to hide any more.

And perhaps he is too tired to want to hide any longer.

Alright!

This isn't how it ends.

This might be the nice, easy ending I want you all to see, but I'm sorry, he's right.

(*Confused – writing and performing your own story does that to you.*) I'm right?!

Joel, can we get the house lights on, please?

The lights come up on both him and the audience, and he sees the state of the stage.

It's like coming down after the high of a house party to clean up.

What a fucking mess.

Then suddenly with purpose he pushes one of the boxes back and gets the letters down that have been hanging in the space.

There's another letter in here.

It's fourteen years too late.

I wrote it in late 2017 after, well, after what you just witnessed here tonight.

Fourteen years of living in shame.

Well, here it is.

This is me.

I fucked it up.

Repeatedly.

And do you know what?

That's okay.

Because we all make a mess of our lives.

He points to people in the audience:

You're going to make a mess of yours.

You're going to make a mess of yours.

You're going to make a mess of yours.

And you?

You're going to royally screw yours up.

And you know what?

That's okay.

You're enough.

Four letters.

To say:

He falters, a lump in his throat, this is really hard to say.

I'm sorry it took me so long to say it out loud.

A declaration:

I'm HIV+, and I have been for a very long time.

He goes and gives the letters to four people in the audience.

I want you to know that I'm sorry.

And you to know that I'm sorry.

And you.

And you.

Make sure you take these home and read them.

I posted these to my family in November 2017.

I'd just been commissioned to write a show about my life story and I guess they kind of needed to know.

(*Gesturing to the lighting rig*.) That spotlight comes in useful sometimes.

The day after, my brother and sister-in-law and my mum came over.

Mum brought a house plant, like you do.

She said she probably already knew, just like when I came out at sixteen.

Mother's intuition.

Then in December 2017, George House Trust asked if I'd speak at the World AIDS Day vigil in Sackville Gardens.

And this time, I could say yes.

No more actors.

And for the *first time*, I could invite my family along.

A brief smile.

My brothers and sisters came.

Mum and Dad didn't.

The smile fades.

He gets the mic and mic stand.

The spotlight resumes.

Music plays: eighties upbeat, hopeful synths.

I wrote a poem for the World AIDS Day vigil in 2017.

Then performed it in this show's premiere in Manchester on World AIDS Day exactly one year later.

A wide smile spreads across his face.

And, I'm pleased to say, Mum and Dad came that time.

Okay, he's in the driving seat now, and you know what? It feels really good.

This is an ending I'm happy with.

And this is the ending you're going to get.

The music swells to the end, perfectly timed with the text.

It's called: 'HOPE, it's just four little letters'.
Hope
It's just four little letters
H, O, P and E
Just four little letters
Folded inside four little envelopes.

And there he stands
Four letters in hand
Before the red postbox that brings hope
After fourteen years
Of living in fear
One drop
And it's finally done.

Four letters to try and explain
Why shame
Led to silence
Led to sadness
Led to hopelessness.

The space begins to fill with red light, including the neon triangle.

But you see
None of us are getting out of this alive
You can fight and scream and strive
To deny the inevitable end
But it will come
And there's nothing to be done about it.

And some days, it won't just rain
It will pour down.
And all around you you'll see hopelessness.

But who said rain had to stop play, hey?
Lord only knows, if we let a little light drizzle
Fizzle out our flames
In Manchester
Well, we'd never get any partying done.

And, you can still dance in the rain, right?

He clicks his fingers and the mirror ball starts spinning.

He's taking control back: of his life, of the story, of the show, of the pure theatrics of it all.

The music swells.

Every good friend of Dorothy knows
That somewhere after the stormy shit-show of a show
Is somewhere over the rainbow
It's fucking cheesy
But it's true
No use feeling blue
For too long, our kid.

So, come rain or shine
I'll carry my little letters with pride.

And HOPE...
It's just four little letters.
H, O, P and E.

No big deal
Just four little letters
Each one sealed
Tight with the regret and remorse
Of nearly fifteen years of silence.

Yet a moment more still he lingers
The paper squeezed tightly between his fingers
Before dropping four little letters
To Sister, Brother, Father, Mother...
To say...

The music climaxes and ends.

A few heavy breaths in the silence.

It's just *three* little letters.

Blackout.

Curtain call.

And then, a final, private moment…

Moment 17:
A Letter

The following letter is handed in a sealed envelope to each
audience member as they leave the auditorium. It is an exact
copy of the letter that Nathaniel sent to his family members.

Dear Mum and Dad,

There is something I need to reach out and tell you, but every
time I try and say it out loud, nothing comes out. So I'm writing
it down.

I am HIV+ and have been for a long time.

I caught the virus from the first time I had sex – talk about
unlucky. I found out about two weeks after my seventeenth
birthday.

For years I have lived with toxic shame controlling me and I no
longer want to do so. For years I thought keeping it inside was
somehow staying in control, but over recent years the anxiety
and sadness this has caused me has become unbearable.

The most ridiculous thing is that I am 100% fit and well – I take
a tablet before bed and visit the clinic twice a year. Studies
suggest people living with HIV will live longer lives than those
who don't and the condition has been downgraded to long-term-
manageable status alongside asthma and diabetes.

But unlike other conditions, the shame and stigma attached to
the virus is massive. It's so massive that even a seemingly
confident and resilient person like myself has struggled to be
open about it with those closest to me.

When you realise you are gay there is a mountain to climb to
come out – you can't underestimate what it feels like to realise
that you're fundamentally different to everyone you know (at
the time) and that for all the leaps and bounds in equality and
acceptance, the world is profoundly homophobic.

You live in a world where you have to constantly check your
surroundings and the people you speak to: is it safe to out

myself in this environment? Can I hold my partner's hand here
without someone shouting abuse... or worse? And almost
weekly you hear stories of friends or people in the community
who've been attacked or you read of young people taking their
own lives because school was unbearable. It's why I've always
tried to be as visible and open as a gay man and why I've
always been drawn to help other LGBT people.

But despite many LGBT people's confident exteriors there is a
struggle, a battle with internalised homophobia and shame – I
truly believe this is why rates of depression and suicide are
higher than average for gay men in particular. Over the years
I've had support from teachers, doctors, friends, counsellors and
all have concluded the same.

**And the only way to rid yourself of shame is to walk
towards the fear that causes it.**

When I was diagnosed with HIV it was a different world, a
different diagnosis than it is today. Now, thanks to great work
from activists and campaigners, healthcare provided for people
living with HIV is exemplary and, slowly, attitudes are
beginning to change. When I found out back in 2003, all I knew
was I'd caught an incurable illness.

Remember that Section 28 – Thatcher's Government's
homophobic legislation stopping schools from talking about
homosexuality openly – was in place all of my school life (it
was repealed in 2003, the year I caught the virus). The only
education we got on being gay was a video about a gay man
with AIDS, hardly a great start in life for young gay and bi men
and women.

Fortunately for me it wasn't the very early days of the HIV
crisis and I was told I had a chronic condition with a prognosis
of around 37 years (similar to diabetes) – now, all being well,
I'll be getting just as old and decrepit as everyone else! But just
at the moment where I was becoming so acutely aware of the
struggle ahead as a gay man, another layer of shame and fear
was added. And I closed it off and buried it away and pretended
that ignoring it would somehow stop me feeling ashamed at

what I'd done, what I'd got. As though having sex with someone was a shameful thing to do.

Of course, it didn't stop me feeling ashamed. It only got worse and manifested itself in bouts of sadness and depression, in constant anxiety and a striving to make things, make life perfect to try and cover up my shame.

I've not lived in complete silence. Of course some close friends know, and lovers. I received amazing support at college and university from staff and counsellors as well as George House Trust. Perhaps, in a sense it was too good because I didn't need to turn to the people closest to me for support... or I thought I didn't.

Of course, the big question in your mind will be: but why didn't he tell us when he knows we'd be loving and accepting? The honest answer? I don't know. Often the perception of fear is worse than the fear itself. And there never seemed a right time – time with family always seemed so precious. Believe me I have tried more times than I can recall, but each time the words stuck in my throat.

In recent years as I've grown and matured I've begun to recognise the root cause of my anxieties and have realised that continuing to bury my shame, my fear, my true self will only result in further sadness, anger and resentment at the world.

And so it's time to come out the closet again.

More and more I've felt compelled to tackle this ridiculous shame and fear that plagues so many people's lives, particularly those with HIV. Whilst we may have all caught it in different ways, the stories I've heard in support sessions with other people with the virus are all the same: the stigma attached is so great that we choose to stay quiet. Not any more.

I'm also facing up to my responsibilities and actions over the past fifteen years – I have to own the choices I've made, the lies I've told and the hurt they may have caused and say sorry for that, to you and other people.

I know for you this will be difficult and you'll be feeling anger, sadness, confusion – a whole host of things – but I know that those feelings will pass. Oddly, for me, it is kind of ancient history.

As you know, I've always been a passionate activist and advocate for HIV and LGBT rights. More recently I've been using theatre, writing and poetry to help me make sense of everything and I've shared some of this with colleagues and peers and fellow artists and producers. They have offered support to help me develop my own show/project around this – it feels right for me at this time in my life.

So over the coming months I will be working towards this. And whilst there is an urgency to tell those closest to me the full truth before this, this isn't the reason why I am telling you now, it's all just part of the journey to full disclosure. And I want you to share in that journey too. Why the hell wouldn't I?!

I know you'll have a million questions – please ask, reach out. I just wasn't sure I could go through this conversation with each family member and not have a mini emotional breakdown in the process.

I'm not sure what else I can say at this point other than I love you all very much.

Nathaniel xxx

Workshops and Activities

A note on working with autobiographical material

Many of the scenes in *First Time* describe old memories in vivid detail – but the process of recalling the past can be painful. When writing the play I used a few different techniques to try and rediscover the past memories, both traumatic and joyous.

Remember that when you are making work from your own experience it is important to ask yourself if you are comfortable sharing things publicly. Keep asking yourself this question, reassessing your answer and adjusting your process accordingly.

I had a good amount of professional support (including professional therapy) during the development of *First Time*, and whilst, for me, being brutally honest about my past has been an overwhelmingly positive experience, it can be risky (and even unethical) to work in this way with people who are not ready.

This is particularly true when working in educational settings. Whilst it is important to encourage students to reflect on the challenging aspects of life, workshops should focus on using *existing* text or drama. Anything autobiographical should be 'light touch' and focus more on generalised shared challenges, hopes, dreams and fears.

One of the benefits of exploring through writing and drama is that you can introduce elements that aren't true, or anonymise people's writing to use in workshops or performance, although this comes with its own set of ethical and safeguarding challenges.

My advice is to think and plan carefully before embarking on any autobiographical work – both with yourself or with a group you are directing. Ask yourself the questions: why you are doing this, and what purpose does it serve?

Always make sure you have the permission of someone to use their words (even if anonymous), and always make sure you are clear with them how and where you will use them.

Finally, continually 'check in' on the well-being of yourself and others whilst doing this type of work, and remember: it's not all doom and gloom, life has many joyous moments worth celebrating too!

Workshop 1:
Bringing a Memory to Life on the Page and Onstage

This workshop explores how therapeutic 'recall memory' techniques can be used in the process of creating theatre.

Read

• Moments 2, 3, 4, 5 and 6 in *First Time*.
  These scenes travel through many different places and times, sometimes jumping between times and places within a scene itself.

Explore

• How does the writer/performer transport us to new places and times?
• What do they use to do this? (Think about: props, music, costume, textual references – e.g. a Nokia 5210 mobile phone tells us the era we are in.)
• How do they communicate how they are feeling? (Think about: stage directions, speech patterns, lighting, sound.)

Discuss

• What elements of these scenes really grab your attention?
• How does the writer/performer help you keep up? (For example: they tell you directly where they are and what the weather is.)
• How do we learn other things about the writer/performer? (For example: they make snarky comments about the prom, they are visibly shaking at the clinic, they fantasise all the time.)

Try

A teacher or workshop leader can guide people through this exercise.

- Choose a memory that you would like to set a scene in or about. It doesn't have to be a sad or painful one; happy memories can be just as powerful onstage.
- Close your eyes and take some deep breaths. Notice everything that distracts you – sounds, the feeling of your clothes – then let them pass through you, trying to empty your mind.
- Once settled, imagine the place where the memory happened. There are a few ways people like to do this:
  - Like a film. You are sat watching the memory on a big screen in front of you and can pause, rewind and fast-forward.
  - Like a 'POV' computer game. You inhabit an avatar of yourself re-entering the space, and you can explore by walking around.
  - Like *The Sims*. There is an avatar of yourself, but instead of being inside this character and viewing the world from their eyes, you hover slightly above and observe what they do.
- Now take some time to explore the memory – really map out the space in your mind. What can you see, hear, smell, taste, touch?
- Walk about, be curious: what is through that door? Inside that magazine? Round that corner?
- Take time to notice how you feel in your body. Are you nervous? Tense? Buzzing with excitement? At peace? Happy?
- When ready, take some time to leave the space you've created in your mind. Stop the film, power down the computer – and slowly refocus your mind on the present space and sounds (don't rush this part).
- Once you have fully returned to the here and now, immediately write down everything you could see, smell, hear, taste and touch. Take some time to document your feelings and emotions too.

- Share your experience with others (only as much as you are comfortable with).

Create

Using the notes you have made, write the opening to a scene that will document the memory. The description of the clinic in Moment 6 was written using this technique.

Remember the techniques you discovered in the *First Time* script:

- Direct address.
- Remarks that reveal character and their state of mind.
- Props and costume.
- Lighting and sound (including music).
- Stage directions.
- Don't forget that theatre is a visual medium. Where you can, show your audience rather than telling them!

Go Further

The writer/performer dramatises this 'recall' technique in Moment 11 when they watch a version of their painful past on a TV screen whilst high on drugs.

- How have they dramatised the technique and brought it to life onstage?
- Is it clear if this is a real memory or not?
- How and why does the writer/performer explores this memory in such a way?
- How has the writer/performer distorted reality in order to explore the repetitious and debilitating effects of post-traumatic stress?

Workshop 2:
Using Verbatim Text

'Verbatim' is the process of using real words in a creative work – they may be your own or someone else's. There are many different types of verbatim theatre. Some people like to recreate the words as faithfully as possible; others use the words creatively to make poetry, prose, dialogue or songs.

Read

• Moment 7 in *First Time*.

Discuss

• How does this list differ from the first half of the play?
• Why is it so different in style and tone?
• What dramatic purposes does this scene have? (For example: demonstrates many years of life have passed, reveals things the writer/performer is ashamed of, provides social and political context – e.g. Section 28.)
• The writer/performer says the list is 'in no particular order', but do you think they have edited it in a certain way?
• Why do you think they may have edited it?

Try

• Each statement on the list is like the beginning of a story we never get to hear. Choose one (or a few) and write, improvise or create a piece of poetry, theatre or dance that imagines the story we haven't heard.
• Try to craft a story or narrative using the verbatim statements. You could even try to place them into a poem or set them to music.

Create

- Gather verbatim material on a topic or theme and explore different ways to present the words. Remember to be clear with people what your intentions with their words are before you begin.
- Ask everyone in your group to complete an agreed sentence on slips of paper (for example: 'When he was younger he...' / 'In the end they...' / 'She never thought...'). Gather them in and use the material to inspire creative writing or drama.

Go Further

- Older or more experienced groups may want to do the previous exercise with true-life confessions anonymously. These do not need to be dark or traumatic, they can be uplifting, cheeky and funny. A strong bond of trust is required, and drama leaders should carefully consider their safeguarding practices when working in this manner.
- Discuss the ethics of using your own or other people's words verbatim when creating dramatic work.

Workshop 3:
Using Live or Performance Art Techniques

First Time is not a monologue from beginning to end, and utilises many different live-art and performance-art techniques.

Read

- Moments 4, 5, 7, 9, 10 and 11 in *First Time*.

Discuss

- What creative techniques has the writer/performer used in the scenes? (For example: lip-syncing, a quiz, playing with party ephemera.)
- Why have they chosen to use these at these moments?
- How effective do you think these ideas are for capturing a feeling or telling parts of the story?

Try

- Lip-syncing is an art form utilised by drag artists, often with popular cultural references and songs telling over-the-top stories full of camp and melodrama.
- In *First Time*, the writer/performer lip-syncs to a song that has significance to their past whilst wallowing in self-pity with a breakfast of drugs.
- Choose a moment from a play or story, then choose a song that a character could 'sing' at that moment. Think about how lyrics may take on new meanings or how you could contrast serious drama with high camp or comedy.
- Try lip-syncing as the character or characters. How can you tell a story through the lip-sync? (It's not as easy as it first looks!)

- Experiment with tone and style. What happens if you use a pop song in a classical play, or have opera in the middle of a play set in a school?

Go Further

- Research contemporary theatre-makers and the techniques they use. Try Bryony Kimmings, Scottee, Le Gateau Chocolat and Stacy Makishi as starting points.
- Explore your play or project with an extended improvisation with props, costume, music, etc. Operate with a spirit of playfulness and openness, there is no right or wrong when exploring this way, it's all about discovery!

Other Creative Ideas

Write a letter to yourself

The writer/performer speaks about writing a letter to their sixteen-year-old self. If you could speak to yourself in the future or the past, what would you say? Write a letter to yourself – you can keep this private or choose to share with a group.

Use humour to explore difficult topics

First Time uses humour to deal with some difficult themes. Think about scenarios that are difficult or embarrassing and see if you can find the humour in those moments. Television comedies and film often do the same. Can you name any? Watch them for inspiration! Perhaps you could tell some of your own story as a stand-up routine or a slapstick performance.

Write a poem with repetition

The writer/performer uses repetition in much of their work, particularly in their poetry. Read 'First Time' on page xvii and 'HOPE, it's just four little letters' on page 61, and then try and write a poem or prose using repetition in a similar manner.

Other Workshops

The following workshops/outreach projects were developed and are delivered alongside *First Time*. For more information, visit: www.nathanieljhall.co.uk/in-equal-parts

In Equal Parts

In Equal Parts is a community-led creative outreach project tackling HIV stigma and shame. It aims to *educate* everybody – regardless of HIV status – on modern HIV healthcare and prevention, *destigmatise* attitudes to the virus, and *empower* people to understand their role in contributing to the global aim of ending all new HIV transmissions by 2030.

To date, *In Equal Parts* has engaged over 5,500 participants in creative workshops, talks, exhibitions, rapid HIV-testing and fundraising parties, and over 18,000 people online. Along with the play, *In Equal Parts* has taken the Undetectable = Untransmittable (U=U) and Zero 2030 campaign messages to millions in broadcast, digital and print media.

ACTUP+Live

We're on a mission to end all new transmissions of HIV across the UK by 2030 – it's hugely ambitious, but if we all work together, it's achievable.

ACTUP+Live is an upbeat, creative, educational workshop offered by Dibby Theatre as a free digital resource to schools and youth groups. The hands-on session aims to raise awareness of HIV healthcare, prevention and stigma through the lens of HIV activism past, present and future. It explores how everyday art and creativity has inspired social and political change, and educates and empowers young people to take responsibility for their sexual health.

In educational settings, *ACTUP+Live* is suitable for Key Stage 3, 4 and beyond – delivering learning outcomes for PSHE, SRE, the Humanities, History and Art. It is offered as a free digital workshop with pre-recorded teaching film and digital resources to support delivery. Participants are challenged to make their own artwork suitable for the #Zero2030 generation – and invited to share this work on a digital 'quilt' of HIV art activism on Nathaniel's website.

Support and Services

Regular testing (once a year) for HIV is recommend for anyone who is sexually active. Those who are not regularly using protection or have casual partners should test every three months.

There is a range of testing options, including home-testing kits. To find out more, and to find how to get tested near to you, visit: www.nhs.uk/conditions/hiv-and-aids/diagnosis

PrEP (Pre-Exposure Prophylaxis) is an effective method for reducing the risk of contracting HIV – speak to your healthcare professional for further advice.

Condoms also remain an effective method for reducing the risk of transmission.

People living with HIV who are on effective medication cannot pass on the virus to their sexual partners.

George House Trust – the official charity partner of *First Time*

GHT offer a range of support and advocacy services for people living with or affected by HIV in the North West of England. 0161 274 4499 | www.ght.org.uk

Terrence Higgins Trust

The UK's leading HIV and sexual-health charity with services across London, the south-west and the rest of the UK. 0808 802 1221 | www.tht.org.uk

National AIDS Trust

Campaigning and advocacy charity transforming the UK's response to HIV. www.nat.org.uk

National AIDS Map

NAM changes lives by sharing information about HIV and
AIDS, and is an excellent factual resource.
www.aidsmap.com

HIV Scotland – the official charity partner of *First Time* in
Scotland

Supporting people living with and affected by HIV in Scotland,
HIV Scotland are known for their detailed policy work and
successful advocacy.
www.hiv.scot

Prepster

Activist-led organisation aiming to educate and agitate for PrEP
access in England and beyond.
www.prepster.info

LGBT Foundation

LGBT Foundation is a national charity delivering advice,
support and information services to lesbian, gay, bisexual and
trans (LGBT) communities.
www.lgbt.foundation

Mind

Mind is a national charity providing advice and support to
anyone experiencing a mental-health problem. They campaign
to improve services, raise awareness and promote
understanding.
www.mind.org.uk